THE COLORS OF NATURE

# THE COLORS OF NATURE

## SUBTROPICAL GARDENS BY RAYMOND JUNGLES

### FOREWORD BY TERENCE RILEY

THE MONACELLI PRESS

Published in the United States by The Monacelli Press,
a division of Random House, Inc.

The Monacelli Press and the colophon are trademarks of
Random House, Inc.

Library of Congress Cataloging-in-Publication Data
Jungles, Raymond.
The colors of nature : subtropical gardens by Raymond Jungles /
[Raymond Jungles] ; foreword by Terence Riley. — 1st ed.
p.   cm.
ISBN 978-1-58093-212-7
1. Jungles, Raymond. 2. Landscape architects—Florida.
3. Landscape architects—Panama. 4. Landscape architecture—
Florida. 5. Landscape architecture—Panama. I. Title.
SB470.J86A3   2008
712.092—dc22                          2008024213

Printed in China

10987654321
First edition

Designed by Think Studio, NYC

www.monacellipress.com

# FOREWORD

In his 1878 novel *The Europeans*, Henry James chronicles the experiences and personalities of a family of proper New Englanders and their visiting Continental relatives, who dazzled and perplexed their Yankee cousins with their worldliness. James himself had been living in Europe for ten years when he wrote the book, and its autobiographical perspective is obvious. A memorable line, which sums up the book's view of America, describes the New England countryside: "the uncastled landscape."

While American tastes and traditions vary widely, the open landscape—unbounded by fences or walls and uncrowned by castles, churches, or villas—has proven to be a consistent national ideal, rendered by painters and captured by photographers from Thomas Cole to Ansel Adams. By contrast, Europe was then and is now justly famous for the culture that has produced an entire vocabulary of landscape design, from the formal parterres of Versailles to the romantic inventions of Capability Brown's eighteenth-century parks. Indeed, aspects of these gardens and parks were imported to the Americas along with other elements of European culture and remain influential still. As recently as the 1970s, John Paul Getty commissioned a Pompeian villa with traditional European gardens for his home in Malibu.

However, the truly American contribution to landscape design—the cultural equivalent to that of Europe—can be seen in Teddy Roosevelt's setting aside of 194 million acres of wilderness, including the Grand Canyon and Yosemite, as national parks. Roosevelt did not, of course, create these landscapes, but he certainly recognized their beauty and their importance to American culture. Appreciation of the wilderness—the undisturbed natural condition—became a root source of inspiration for generations of American designers who created man-made landscapes that seemed to grow out of nature, from Frederick Law Olmsted's Central Park in New York City to Frank Lloyd Wright's Taliesin West, his 600-acre compound near Phoenix, Arizona.

Perhaps because of its subtropical climate, unique within the North American continent, the Florida landscape is often seen as a separate and distinct chapter in the national fascination with the natural landscape. Yet the same dialectic between European gardening traditions and New World fascination with the wild is at play. Vizcaya, James Deering's Miami estate, was patterned after a grand Italianate villa with attendant formal gardens. While greatly admired, Vizcaya has been far less often imitated as Florida's landscape designers have instead chosen nature—or at least idealized visions of tropical nature—as their prime source of inspiration.

Raymond Jungles, thoroughly entranced by the wild, is one such landscape designer. The intensity with which he approaches his task is related, no doubt, to his exposure to the work and philosophy of the Brazilian artist and designer Roberto Burle Marx (1909–1994). Burle Marx was part of the generation of designers and artists who brought into being in Brazil a vibrant modern culture that has surpassed its European roots and achieved a distinct national character. Perhaps more so than his colleagues, such as the architects Oscar Niemeyer and Lúcio Costa, Burle Marx's innovations achieved a singular distinction, if only because the raw material of his profession—the incomparable flora of Brazil—had no equivalent in Europe or North America. Burle Marx's ability to combine the sensibility of a gardener with that of an abstract modern sculptor is evident in his words: "A garden is a complex of aesthetic and plastic intentions; and the plant is, to a landscape artist, not only a plant—rare, unusual, ordinary or doomed to disappearance—but it is also a color, a shape, a volume or an arabesque in itself."

It was in Burle Marx's work that the young Jungles, a student landscape designer raised primarily in the Midwest, found not only a wealth of knowledge about subtropical plants and a unique aesthetic perspective but, as important, an attitude that provided both an ethical and a humanistic framework for landscape design. For Burle Marx, landscape design was a component of a broader investigation into the culture of the modern world, one without precedent save in nature itself. The extent to which Jungles has absorbed and synthesized these various attitudes is evident in the delicate balance between aesthetic delight and studied naturalism that is characteristic of his work. His promotion of native plant material and other environmentally sound horticultural practices underpins the formal with the ethical. Visitors to Jungles's gardens will also realize that his designs are not simply collections of botanical specimens but places of wonder and exhilaration. It is those attributes that most closely connect Jungles's work to the broader stream of the American attitude toward nature and the wilderness, the "uncastled landscape."

TERENCE RILEY

# DOING WHAT I LIKE

Some of my earliest memories are of natural landscapes and wild animals. Gerry Weber, my stepfather, was an avid outdoorsman raised near the Black Forest in Germany, and he instilled in my mother, Lelah, my brother, Jim, my sister, Laura, and me his love of the natural world. He took us camping and hiking in Yosemite and Sequoia National Parks, diving in Baja California, sailing over the Pacific to Catalina Island, and exploring on the beaches up and down the coast near our home in Long Beach. It's no surprise that the time I spent in these places of incredible scenic majesty shaped what I ended up doing.

Our family, in its various configurations, was always moving. When I was seven, we returned to Omaha, Nebraska, where both my mother and I were born. Jim and I were constantly on the go, biking, hiking, and swimming in the wild areas on the fringes of the city. From Nebraska we went to Illinois, then to Ohio. Camping and playing ice hockey became my main pastimes, and reading—reading about nature, animals, and Native American cultures.

In high school in Columbus, Ohio, I was in the Horticultural Study Program, part of Future Farmers of America. When I was sixteen, I started a summer job at Fozzie's Nursery, and I worked there part-time during my senior year, earning school credits. I played hockey on a traveling team and dreamed about living in the Canadian wilderness—after all, this time coincided with the final years of the Vietnam War. This was also when I first traveled to Miami. A good friend and I rode our motorcycles down one spring break. I was struck by the beaches and bikinis but even more by the vast Florida sky and the wide-open spaces. In 1974, after I graduated, I announced to my mother and sister that I was moving there.

And I did, supporting myself by working as a landscape laborer, learning much about the climate and the value of shade. My boss, John Ross, challenged me to become a mason and a carpenter yet often left me to work out the techniques on my own. He taught me that human relations and enthusiasm are the primary ingredients in building a garden and encouraged me to become a landscape architect.

At that time, the University of Florida, Gainesville, was the only state university that offered a bachelors degree in landscape architecture, and because the landscape architecture program is part of the College of Architecture, I needed some prerequisite classes. It was during these classes that I really started to develop skills in spatial design. My successes in architectural design classes prompted professors and other students to encourage me to pursue a degree in architecture.

But one day a friend in the landscape architecture program showed me *The Tropical Gardens of Roberto Burle Marx*, a book by Pietro M. Bardi. With a brilliantly written introduction and image after image of Burle Marx's gardens, art, and architecture, this book had an immediate impact on me and would inspire me into the future—in fact, it still does. Here was a poet who had chosen to use nature as a means of self-expression. In 1979, Roberto came to Gainesville to lecture. I had been offered a summer job in Caracas, and I arranged with Roberto a trip to Rio to visit his studio. Unfortunately, changing economic conditions in Venezuela eliminated my position, and my visit to Brazil was postponed indefinitely.

Near the end of my studies, I visited California, which felt like the ideal place to start my career—California was always on the cutting edge of landscape architecture. Frank Gehry's buildings and Lawrence Halprin's plazas sparked my imagination; the beaches of La Jolla, Santa Monica, and Malibu seemed to be calling me home. But ongoing projects in Miami, the positive press reviews of my senior thesis, *The Bayfront Park System: A Pedestrian Celebration*, and continuing offers to design and build gardens on my own kept me from relocating.

I wrote to Roberto Burle Marx all through my senior year and as I began my practice after graduation. Then one evening in 1981, Lester Pancoast, a well-known Miami architect and friend of Roberto's, phoned me to say that Roberto was in Miami and wanted to have dinner. Among many other topics of conversation, we determined that I would travel with him from Miami to Rio at the end of his U.S. lecture circuit. At that time, I didn't know that Roberto always brought gifts from his travels to his many friends and employees. I gladly accommodated him when he asked if I had any extra room in my luggage. This was the first time I experienced his legendary generosity. The second was to follow almost immediately: when we cleared customs in Rio, he insisted that I come with him to his home.

So began a friendship and a mentorship that lasted until his death in 1994. I would visit Roberto at least once every year, sharing his home, his life, his friends, and his love of nature. Days were spent watching him paint, work on a sculpture, or plant a new garden on his property. Botanists from around the globe would visit his extensive collection, speaking of plants I had never heard of and exchanging rare species.

Traveling with Roberto around Brazil on business, for exhibitions, or on plant-collecting excursions exposed me to extraordinary natural beauty but also to the destruction of the Brazil he loved and so passionately defended.

I visited Roberto Burle Marx every year for fourteen years at his home, now Sítio Roberto Burle Marx, a botanical garden open to the public; plant-collecting expeditions were a highlight of the annual trips; the chief horticulturalist for Fairchild Tropical Botanic Garden accompanied us one year.

PREVIOUS PAGE Roberto suggested that I design and build a bromeliad column for the Museum of Modern Art's 1991 exhibition of his work.

His celebrity status provided great impetus to the conservation movement. Often he would talk about his moral obligation to fight the arrogance and stupidity of human greed.

Roberto's nature-based aesthetics resonated with my love of the wilderness from childhood, and his encyclopedic knowledge of plants and precision in exploring how each one interacts spoke to my interest in true habitat. Listening to him discuss the gardens he had created and new plans as he mentored his staff, as well as free access to his drawing files and library, helped me construct the vocabulary that would come into play in my own landscape design, whether animating an entry walk for the Montifiore garden or creating the harmonious expanses of the Ward garden.

Working almost exclusively in Florida has also shaped my approach to landscape. I am constantly stimulated by the vibrancy of the indigenous fauna and flora and feel our projects are a success when we create viable natural habitat. A lifestyle that fuses interior and exterior spaces refreshes my spirit, and I know it speaks to many others as well. Our gardens strive for a "clearing in the woods" sense of privacy, so important to many of our clients, and the integration of life and nature.

It may seem easy to address such aspirations in the subtropical climate of Florida; however, nature has its own restrictions here. The uniform, mostly flat topography is not always inspiring, especially since elevation can be crucial for the success of plants, most of which cannot thrive below four feet above sea level. Species must also tolerate strong winds, salt, and the feast-or-famine cycle of rainfall. Landscape designers come up against cultural biases as well. Developers and homeowners generally want dramatic, tropical landscapes consisting of mostly exotic ornamental

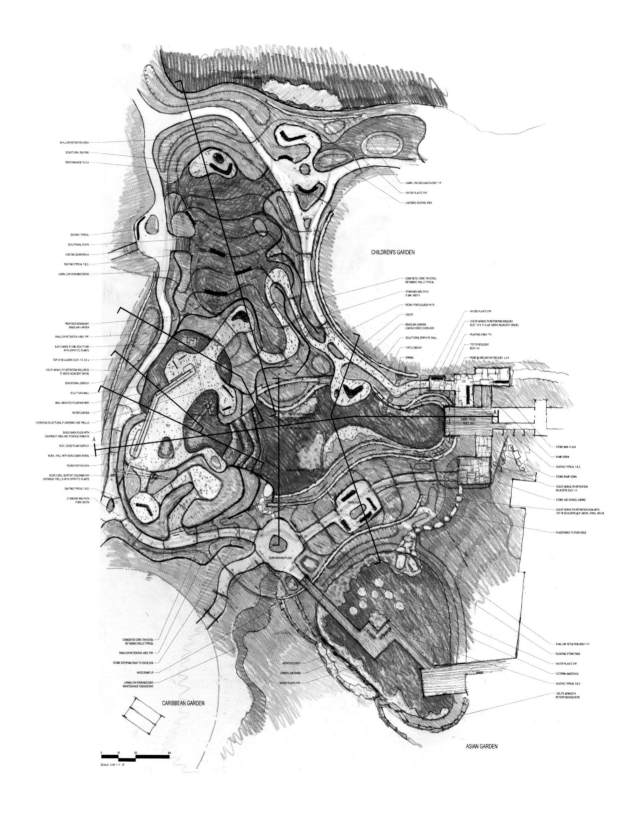

SHALLOW RETENTION AREA
SCULPTURAL SEATING
PERFORMANCE PLAZA

LAWN LOW GROUNDCOVER TYP.
WATER PLANTS TYP.
LAKESIDE SEATING AREA

CHILDREN'S GARDEN

SEATING TYPICAL
SCULPTURAL STEPS
EXISTING BOARDWALK
SEATING TYPICAL T.B.D.
LAWN LOW GROUNDCOVERS

CONCRETE/ CORE TEN STEEL
RETAINING WALLS TYPICAL
STANDARD NBG PATH
8' MIN. WIDTH
PEDRA PORTUGUESA PATH

DOLITE
BRAZILIAN GARDEN
CANTILEVERED OVERLOOK
SCULPTURAL EPIPHYTE WALL
TURTLE BEACH
SPRING

WATER PLANTS TYP.
DOLITE MONOLITH RETENTION BOULDER
ELEV. 10.0-11.5 ±/8" ABOVE ADJACENT GRADE)
PLANTING AREA TYP.
TOP OF BOULDER
ELEV. 4.5
POND @ GROUND WATER ELEV. ± 3.0

PROPOSED BOUNDARY
BRAZILIAN GARDEN
SHALLOW RETENTION AREA TYP.
BURLE MARX STONE SCULPTURE
WITH EPIPHYTIC PLANTS
TOP OF BOULDERS ELEV. 7.5-9.0 ±
DOLITE MONOLITH RETENTION BOULDERS
8" ABOVE ADJACENT GRADE
EDUCATIONAL DISPLAY
SCULPTURAL WALL
WALL MOUNTED FOUNTAIN WEIR
WATER GARDEN
OVERHEAD SCULPTURAL FLOWERING VINE TRELLIS
BURLE MARX PLAZA WITH
EQUIPMENT AREA AND STORAGE BENEATH
SEAT LEDGE/ PLANT DISPLAY
MURAL WALL WITH BURLE MARX MURAL
PEDRA PORTUGUESA
SCULPTURAL SUPPORT COLUMNS FOR
OVERHEAD TRELLIS WITH EPIPHYTIC PLANTS
SEATING TYPICAL T.B.D.
STANDARD NBG PATH
8' MIN. WIDTH

STONE MINI-PLAZA
RAMP DOWN
SEATING TYPICAL T.B.D.
STONE RAMP DOWN
DOLITE MONOLITH RETENTION
BOULDERS ELEV. 4.5
STONE AND GRASS LANDING
DOLITE MONOLITH RETENTION BOULDERS
TOP OF BOULDERS @ 8" ABOVE UPHILL GRADE

FLAGSTONES TO POND EDGE

CONCRETE/ CORE TEN STEEL
RETAINING WALLS TYPICAL
SHALLOW RETENTION AREA TYP.
STONE STEPPING PADS TO OVERLOOK
WOOD RAMP UP
LAWN LOW GROUNDCOVER
MAINTENANCE PASSAGEWAY

SHALLOW RETENTION AREA TYP.
FLOATING STONE PADS
WATER PLANTS TYP.
VICTORIA AMAZONICA
SEATING TYPICAL T.B.D.
DOLITE MONOLITH
RETENTION BOULDERS

WATER PLANTS TYP.
LOWER LAKE BASIN
WATER PLANTS TYP.

CARIBBEAN GARDEN

ASIAN GARDEN

SCALE: 1/16" = 1' - 0"

16

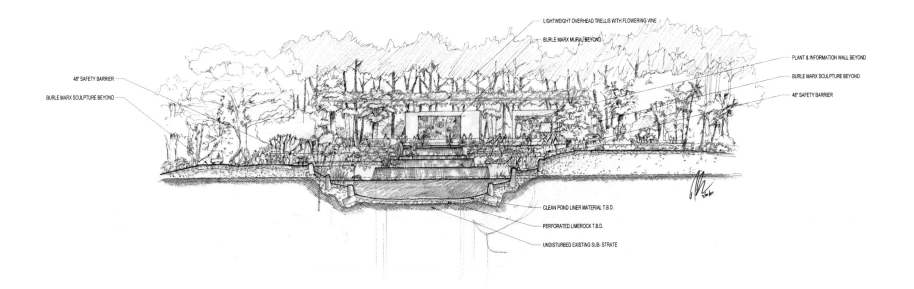

LIGHTWEIGHT OVERHEAD TRELLIS WITH FLOWERING VINE

BURLE MARX MURAL BEYOND

PLANT & INFORMATION WALL BEYOND

BURLE MARX SCULPTURE BEYOND

48" SAFETY BARRIER

48" SAFETY BARRIER

BURLE MARX SCULPTURE BEYOND

CLEAN POND LINER MATERIAL T.B.D.

PERFORATED LIMEROCK T.B.D.

UNDISTURBED EXISTING SUB-STRATE

Our design for the Brazilian Garden at the Naples Botanical Garden is a tribute to Roberto Burle Marx; I donated the ceramic mural from my own collection.

plants that require fertilization, soil amendments, and unnatural precipitation. These landscapes resemble Tahiti, Bali, or Malaysia more than they resemble Florida. We attempt to be true to our unique geographical location, a vast peninsula, once the floor of the ocean, between the Atlantic Ocean and the Gulf of Mexico.

Our gardens promote the use of native plants, creation of habitat, and conservation of the earth's valuable resources. By using species that are encouraged to mature as nature intended, we eliminate the need for countless hours of pruning. We prefer a softer, looser order of plant volumes; gardens that harmonize with local ecosystems; gardens that appear almost subversive. Built interventions are minimal and sculptural, complementing through contrast the soft plantings. Color and texture are generously applied.

But our primary concern is space. All of our designs begin by defining spatial possibilities. Poetic interpretation—"What should it be?" not "What could it be?"—informs our process. We value research but never deny intuition. Time spent on site is critical, and earth forms and plants are typically redrawn and adjusted during installation. In these moments, the third dimension takes on an important role in the creative process. Bringing people closer to nature, creating space that is inspirational, advancing curiosity, knowledge, and appreciation of the relationship between people, nature, and art—these are our goals.

We apply our beliefs to the opportunities we have. In recent years, this has meant hospitality projects, usually in the form of boutique hotels. Designs at the civic scale, which reach many more people than private commissions, are important to us. Like lectures, public projects provide a venue to continue to develop our garden philosophy.

Botanical gardens are a special challenge. Our Brazilian Garden at the Naples Botanical Garden, due to be built in 2009, will be my tribute to Roberto Burle Marx. His love of plants, especially Brazilian plants, was legendary and contagious. His simple, intense, fulfilling lifestyle was unforgettable. In conversations with family, friends, and students, he would advise "Do what you like": be true to yourself, to your passions. It is the best advice I've ever had.

This was the first house we ever bought, and it served as our residence for ten years. When Debra Yates, my former wife, and I moved in, our son, Benjamin, was two and our daughter, Amanda, was a newborn. Debra and I renovated the house and garden over a period of time, as finances allowed, and eventually converted the garage into my design studio.

The house was nestled on a 10,000-square-foot corner lot in a quiet residential neighborhood; the property was shaded by mature canopy trees. We wanted to create privacy using the most economical means possible. One weekend we relocated the large shrubs used as foundation plants to the right-of-way between the street and the side property line. Next, we built a tall fence of wooden posts and corrugated metal sheeting, applying matte black spray paint to tone it down. This gave our back garden instant privacy. To enclose the front garden and create a children's play area, we used an inexpensive black chain-link fence; sabal palms and Jamaican capers complete the buffer. The garden also became a laboratory where we continually introduced plants we brought back from Roberto Burle Marx's garden and nurseries: new philodendrons, bromeliads, palms, and trees.

Besides landscape materials, we explored ideas of fusing interior and exterior spaces. In our Florida room, Debra installed a ceramic mural that continued out the thirty-foot expanse of sliding glass doors and onto the exterior wall of the design studio. The space between two storage sheds became one of three different garden views from my studio. A marine plywood fence enclosing this small area offered a backdrop for an impromptu composition by Debra; a sculptural masonry wall of panels within the densely landscaped easement between our property and the neighbors' displayed her skill as a muralist.

While we lived here, I was able to watch our children grow and experience the joy of outdoor living. Our garden was a haven for raccoons, opossums, birds, and reptiles. We stalked nocturnal creatures with flashlights. Here I learned how intimately a home could be connected to a garden. Hurricane Andrew gave us the opportunity to re-create sections of the garden and make them better. Only the chance to live in Key West could tear us away.

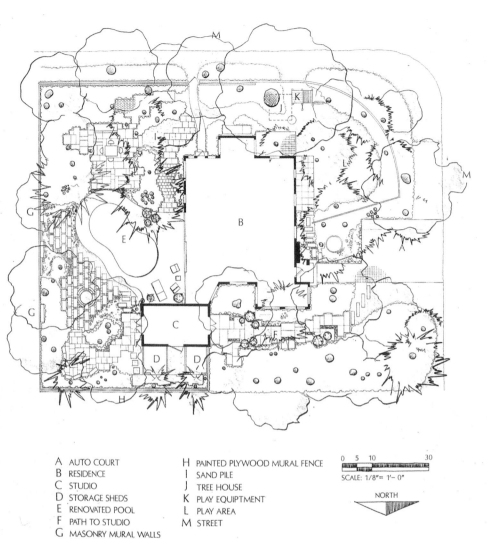

A AUTO COURT
B RESIDENCE
C STUDIO
D STORAGE SHEDS
E RENOVATED POOL
F PATH TO STUDIO
G MASONRY MURAL WALLS

H PAINTED PLYWOOD MURAL FENCE
I SAND PILE
J TREE HOUSE
K PLAY EQUIPTMENT
L PLAY AREA
M STREET

0 5 10 30
SCALE: 1/8"= 1'- 0"

NORTH

Triangle palms and thatch palms shade the auto court and
the main entry to the house; the pool garden is to the east
of the house and the play area to the west; a mineral patina
unifies new concrete pavers and the existing pool deck.

PREVIOUS PAGE A path of recycled pavers
leads to the pedestrian gate.

The tree house is perched on a recycled radio antenna;
Debra Yates created the mural in the pool garden, and
I designed the concrete furniture.

*Portea petropolitana* from Brazil stand alongside a double oak tree; colorful species spring from an elevated, six-foot diameter concrete pot; the studio looks east into the garden.

# LANDES GARDEN

This garden for Catalina Echeverria-Landes was an ongoing collaboration with the client, a South American interior designer, and the architect, Carlos Zapata. Carlos was full of ideas, suggesting directions for pools with glass walls, light-penetrating forms, and structural poetry. The three of us worked together on the hardscape design. Rectangular stone slabs for the auto court repeat the forms of the translucent onyx west facade of the building and the solid stainless-steel panels on the auto gate.

We chose plantings to complement the sculptural qualities of the architecture. Relationships of scale in particular were critical. We strove to be simple and bold and kept the harsh environment of heavy salt spray and howling winds constantly in mind. Catalina desired a relaxed look, not a contrived, eye-catching one. She would say, "Make it look thrown."

We created privacy on the north, south, and west with sabal palms, sea grapes, gumbo limbos, bamboo, and various shade-tolerant understory plants. This perimeter became the "edge of the woods." To the east, we planted the fifty feet of beach with indigenous dune species. The effect we aspired to throughout was art in nature.

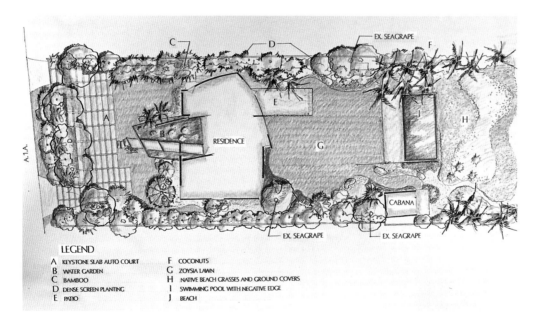

## LEGEND

A    KEYSTONE SLAB AUTO COURT
B    WATER GARDEN
C    BAMBOO
D    DENSE SCREEN PLANTING
E    PATIO
F    COCONUTS
G    ZOYSIA LAWN
H    NATIVE BEACH GRASSES AND GROUND COVERS
I    SWIMMING POOL WITH NEGATIVE EDGE
J    BEACH

The plan features areas of dense native plantings;
in and around the water garden are bamboo, dioons,
and water plants; the plantings and hardscape are
casual in appearance; the view from the beach to
the house includes the pool and zoysia lawn.

PREVIOUS PAGE Roberto Burle Marx's gardens in
Brazil influenced Carlos Zapata's water garden.

Native spider lily borders the pool; the interior and the exterior are separated by a minimal glass plane; the water garden softens the entry.

Catalina Echeverria-Landes designed the furniture
for the palm-shaded sitting area; the view from
the cabana takes in the pool, directly to its north;
the dune was planted to create the impression
that it had always been there.

# JULIE AND JEFF CORNFELD GARDEN

Julie and Jeff Cornfeld, a couple with great appreciation of design and architecture, were working with noted regional architect Don Singer to design a modern two-story residence on their nearly one-acre waterfront site. We were asked to conceptualize the entry sequence and pool configuration as well as design a distinctive garden. It was important to address privacy and security and, of course, to showcase the architecture.

The new house felt large and imposing on the site, which had no trees to mediate the scale of the building. In addition, the garage was overly prominent. We took advantage of the corner lot by angling the driveway in from the northwest corner of the property between two four-foot-high limestone planters. By aligning the pavement with the geometry of the building, we subtly guide visitors to the front door. A mass of bamboo softens the angular lines of the structure.

For the auto court, rock-salt-finished cast-in-place concrete pavers are offset with zoysia grass strips in a pattern that complements the architecture while imparting a human scale. Numerous native canopy trees combined with Cuban sabal palms shade this area and provide shielding from the street. For color, masses of bromeliads surround the bases of trees and tumble from the canopies and trunks, as they do in their native environment. This dense, shady space is the preferred play area for the Cornfelds' young children.

At the front entrance, we extended the interior travertine floor over the platform steps, which we pulled away from the building's walls. The garden reaches out from the voids between steps and walls to envelop the visitor. In the back of the house, the travertine floor extends onto the pool deck. We floated Singer's pool form six inches above the ground, giving it the appearance of a massive cantilever. Water flows continuously from pool to spa; the two basins are separated only by a small ledge containing a flush-mounted fountain jet.

Large-scale silver Bismarck palms, which cast dramatic silhouettes on the dark water of the adjacent lake, provide a foil to the scale of the building. Between the pool and seawall we contoured the grade, keeping areas for the children to play while directing storm water to on-site storage areas. To maintain open water views and intimate garden spaces, we gave priority to indigenous plants in beds of contrasting greens and silvers, highlighted with patches of strong color. We blurred the east and west boundaries of the property to make the site resemble a clearing in the woods. Native trees and understory shrubs establish habitat.

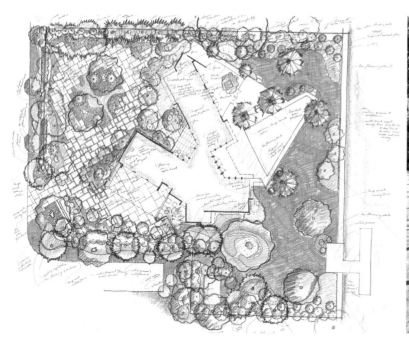

The various wings of the house face distinct garden experiences;
keystone walls in the auto court double as planters;
travertine veneers entry steps, pool deck, and interior floors.

PREVIOUS PAGE Emerald bamboo screens the garage.

Among the plants in the front garden are silver saw palmettos, gumbo limbos, and climbing *Philodendron wilsonii;* the area between the platform steps and the auto court is a favorite play space.

Only one inch of water covers the ledge between pool
and spa; the master bedroom looks out over the pool;
mature Bismarck palms shade pool and deck.

# VICTORIA AND STEPHEN MONTIFIORE GARDEN

Miami Beach, Florida | 1997–1998

New York City dwellers Stephen Montifiore and Victoria DiNardo-Montifiore came to us for a garden for their new winter home in Miami Beach. The plant-loving couple had covered their Chelsea rooftop garden and every windowsill in their apartment with plants. For the new house they wanted to create a three-quarter-acre garden of rich botanical interest. Avid fans of midcentury modern objects, they saw great potential for the 1950s-era structure to complement their extensive collections.

Our first task was to focus on establishing a new approach to the house, one that starts at the drive and continues via the entry walk and a sculptural bridge to the house and pool terrace. The building's close proximity to the front property line dictated maintaining two auto gates and the circular flow of the existing driveway to accommodate numerous vehicles. Striving always to mitigate the impact of automobiles on the garden, we repeated the pattern, geometry, and material of the pool deck, though not at the same scale, for the driveway. The entry walk's cast-concrete pavement extends through the drive, initiating the journey to the front door.

A colorful concrete bridge passes over the water garden. Aquatic plants expand the palette, while the reflective surface and fish animate the space. Passing through this garden room, open to the sky, makes for an enriching entry experience and evokes the spirit of Roberto Burle Marx's nature-based aesthetics.

Access to the pool and dock from the generous covered terrace utilizes the same material, pattern, and scale of the entry walk. We fragmented the pavement to allow the lawn to invade, linking the hardscape and landscape. Bold-scale Bismarck palms define and shade the pool area, while coconut palms overlook a sandy pocket beach.

More tropical in appearance than many of our new gardens, the array of plant material includes numerous Florida natives. The overall garden ambience, siting on the bay, and beautifully renovated modern residence work together to create a distinctive atmosphere. The property is so quintessentially Miami that it was featured in the recent film version of *Miami Vice*.

Cast-concrete pavers lead to a concrete bridge and then to the front door; native Everglades palms impart a natural feel to the water garden; native black ironwood provides both dark green foliage and colorful new growth.

PREVIOUS PAGE The plants between the lawn and the pocket beach—sea purslane, aloe vera, bromeliads, Mexican bush sage, and bulbine—enjoy the sun, need little water, and satisfy our clients' desire for succulents.

In the pocket beach are giant red bromeliads and, by the hammock, *Aechmea* 'Dean'; the sculptural presence of the bridge stands against the soft volumes of the landscape.

A new covered terrace, designed by Glen Heim,
complements the original design of the residence;
coconut palms, formerly scattered over the property,
were relocated to shade the pocket beach.

# SPANISH TROPICAL GARDEN

Our clients had commissioned a family recreational pavilion and lap pool with spa, and architect William Bialosky chose to articulate the new building in what he describes as the contemporary Spanish style. Environmental artist Jackie Ferrara designed the patterns of travertine veneer for all vertical surfaces of the walls and columns.

Our charge was to blend the disparate architectural styles of the 1930s Spanish Colonial main house and the new structure and to detail the garden's paths, grottoes, gates, walls, and terraces. We also decided to revisit the recently installed garden between the residence and the quiet private road. Suburban in nature, the front yard consisted of a circular driveway crowding the entrance and foundation plantings obscuring the character and detailing of the grand residence. Two date palms lent to the driveway's island a stiff formality that ignored the nearby towering Honduran mahogany.

We liberated the facade of the residence, creating an expansive space between it and the street by replacing the circular driveway with a green plaza, contemporary and minimal. The detailing repeats the travertine and patterns of the interiors and terraces. The Honduran mahogany is balanced by two large sculptural South American oil palms; these were sold by a collector to finance his purchase of a pair of breeding Komodo dragons.

We replaced the existing gate with a mahogany door leading to the side and rear gardens. Detailed on top as a planter, this establishes a portal enveloped by lush tropical plantings. Next we added a new terrace to ease the transition from the covered patio adjacent to the center atrium of the house and the vast new side garden. A large stretch of lawn, graded to shed heavy rains, occasionally accommodates tables and a tent.

Huge existing oak trees mitigate the stylistic differences between the contemporary recreational pavilion and the colonial residence. Additional dense multilevel understory palms amend the oaks, gradually thinning from the residence to allow more transparency. Pathways, walls, and detailing of the spa and water garden are all of the same oolite limestone found on the historic columns and arches along the road. Fish and reflections animate the water garden in which the spa floats, and soothing sounds emanate from quiet waterfalls.

An enormous spider sculpture by Louise Bourgeois is integral to the garden. Sited to appear tucked into the jungle's edge, it provides the humor that can be so important in a garden. We underplanted the sculpture with variegated spider plants and provided narrow paths to lure future victims within its reach.

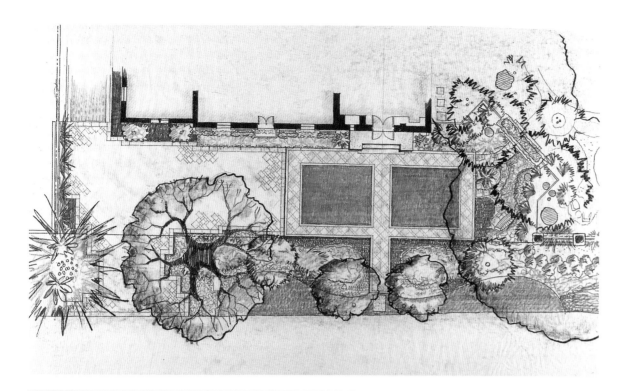

We replaced the canopy tree shown in the plan for the front garden with two American oil palms; *Encephalartos ferox* and *Aechmea blanchetiana* 'Orange Form' provide drought-tolerant texture to the front garden; the sculptural forms of the oil palms balance the scale of the residence.

PREVIOUS PAGE Subtle changes of texture and color balance this "edge of the jungle."

OVERLEAF A mahogany door leads from the front to the side and back gardens; an old man palm was introduced from Cuba; the plan for the rear garden shows the entertainment pavilion and the event lawn; strong hardscape sets off loose plantings.

The clean lines of William Bialosky's pavilion hold one side of the event lawn; the arch patterns on the pool wall, designed by Jackie Ferrara, refer to historic arches on the property; the water garden, complete with island, waterfalls, and floating spa, also supports turtles and fish.

The Florida Keys are a chain of small islands terminating at Key West, less than ninety miles from Cuba. Many of South Florida's urban dwellers escape here for weekends or holidays, drawn by brilliant waters, remnants of unspoiled woodlands, and a laid-back lifestyle. Our clients purchased this seven-acre property for all these reasons, plus a love of fishing on the backwater flats.

Our initial visit with architects Steve Siskind and Bruce Carlson found the site to be mostly barren. A grove of coconut palms had been planted near a colorful two-story bungalow, which was serving as a temporary fish camp. A few mature green buttonwood trees and a tall ficus hedge provided the only green on the bulk of the property. However, the oceanfront property was perfect for a passionate fisherman and his family. A generous boat basin had been excavated, providing hundreds of feet of potential dock protected from storms by a breakwater. Red mangroves had colonized the periphery of this area.

In the Florida Keys, the success of plants depends on elevation above sea level, tolerance of salt and wind, and ability to go long periods of time without rain. Plants indigenous to the Keys grow in thick masses called hammocks. Nestled together for protection from storm-generated winds, their roots intertwine for support, often in shallow soil on top of the fossilized coral reef, also known as keystone. Our desire was to create a garden that would appear to be a natural hammock, accented in areas with subtropical plants that could thrive with little care. We also elevated vast portions of the site, since only a limited number of species survive at less than four feet above sea level.

The garden was started several years before the main house and garage/guest cottage were constructed. This gave us time to find mature canopy trees and palms, and the construction of Sugarloaf High School provided an abundance of mature indigenous trees for rescue and planting around the house. Orchids, another of the clients' passions, are attached to the trunks of trees; they also enliven the interiors.

Siskind and Carlson's architecture was designed in the contemporary Florida vernacular style. Sensitively sited and painted in colorful dark tones, the residence fades into the landscape. We gently terraced the approach to the entry level. Walkways and retaining walls are surfaced in weathered keystone monoliths repurposed from the excavation of septic tanks. Oceanside, a thatched-roof wall-less structure opens onto a play lawn. Dune plantings protect a generous beach complete with a fire circle for nighttime storytelling.

Everything is casual; the driveway and all the paths are of the same material as the beach. This finely crushed keystone is raked regularly. The garden's ambience is hypnotic, a slice of paradise on earth—so much so that it is routinely used as a location for fashion photography, commercials, and films.

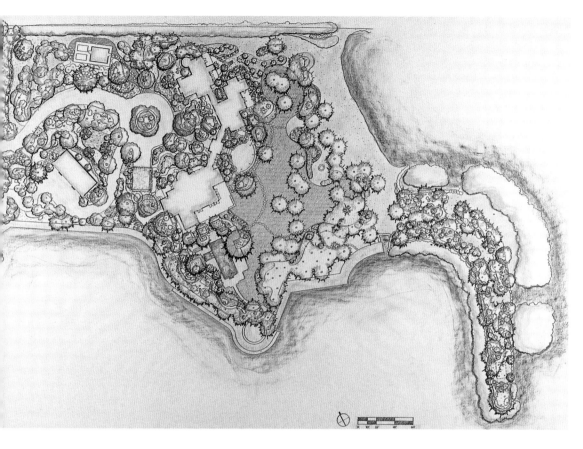

The plan shows the dense native plantings that conceal adjacent residences; the approach road passes through newly created hammocks; the new hammock consists of indigenous trees such as gumbo limbo, mahogany, and strangler fig with an understory punctuated by blooming bromeliads, coontie, and ferns.

PREVIOUS PAGE Dune sunflower helps control erosion, conceals shallow retention areas, thrives in the harsh environment, and provides festive yellow flowers.

Green and silver thatch palms, blolly trees, bromeliads, and wart fern envelop the covered passage between the public and private wings of the house; a gumbo limbo grove, visible through the entry door, resembles the native landscape of the Florida Keys; orchids are grown and recycled into the garden from a structure designed by Siskind and Carlson.

OVERLEAF Rescued native hammock trees and keystone create an ordered yet primitive look; an orchid grows on a native lignum vitae tree.

A narrow path points toward the distant open ocean;
beach bonfires and fish tales go hand in hand.

PREVIOUS PAGES Coconut palms and Fiji Island
fan palms shade the beach by the boat basin.

# JUNGLES/YATES GARDEN

My former in-laws built this residence in Key West in the early 1940s. For many years, Debra Yates and I installed in their garden special plants from our Brazil trips and Fairchild Tropical Botanical Gardens and also indigenous species from the Florida Keys.

My father-in-law, Earl, passed away before we were married. When we were faced with the sudden loss of my mother-in-law, Eva, a witty, much-loved third-generation conch (Key West local), we decided to preserve the residence and renovate it in a cost-effective way. First we built a pool, refurbished the bathrooms and kitchen, and replaced all the plumbing and wiring. The sale of our Miami home allowed us to make further improvements: walls, fences, pergolas, and the installation of a ceramic mural. This mural was part of a series, one of which was displayed at the Venice Biennale. Roberto Burle Marx and his right-hand man, Haruyoshi Ono (Haru has kept Roberto Burle Marx Ltd. going since 1994), worked together on the mural's design. We continued with more construction, converting windows into sliding doors, to allow the space to expand to the planes of the garden's sculptural walls, and pulling interior walls away from exterior walls, to permit the penetration of light.

Budget was always an issue, and we constantly looked for inexpensive ways to accommodate our vision. We reused bricks, washing them with paint to tone them down. We extended the pool tile over the shell to double as coping. Fences were built of marine plywood and recycled timbers from the demolition of a client's roof. We hand-laid leftover Mexican stone from a downtown Miami bank, building on bagged sand that cost more than the stone. We constructed other patios from various project rejects, often turned upside down and installed with the weathered side up. The parking court/basketball court and the front porch are large slabs of concrete with a rock-salt-textured surface and a mineral patina.

Plantings were more tropical than subsequent gardens due to the dense canopies of existing exotic trees and the abundance of plants from Brazil. This project was a labor of love. Although I no longer live there, it brings great satisfaction to know that Debra, Benjamin, and Amanda still have the opportunity to enjoy this piece of family history.

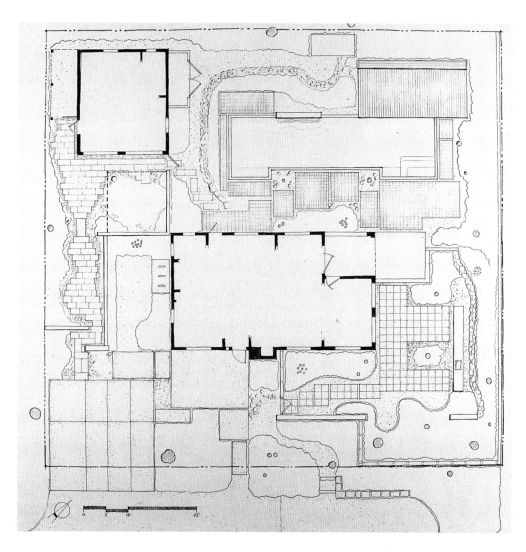

The site plans shows built elements and existing trees, many of which were installed over a long period of time; Roberto Burle Marx and Haruyoshi Ono's mural stands above the pool.

PREVIOUS PAGE The fence along the street was detailed to receive an off-the-shelf mahogany door.

A Central American cycad provides texture; the main living space has a view of tropical black bamboo; the play of light and shadow enlivens the bold scale of the built elements.

# ANNE AND JACKSON WARD GARDEN

I had been aware of this property, along a well-used scenic highway, for many years. The historic 1920s structure is perched on South Florida's highest ridge and along an ancient Indian trail. After Hurricane Andrew, it sat abandoned among broken remnants of the mango orchard that once graced the two-and-a-half-acre property.

Clients Anne and Jackson Ward wanted a natural, rural garden. We removed the ficus hedge behind the original low limestone perimeter wall, then planted indigenous trees and screening shrubs. In addition, we relocated the entrance to exploit the space created by two sculptural live oaks. The gate is placed fifty feet behind the property line for security and to enable a height exceeding property-line wall restrictions.

One unique program element of foremost importance to the Wards was to create a habitat for their pet hog, Virginia, who had been rescued from a busy nearby intersection. A suckling then, she now weighed more than five hundred pounds. We selected a location midway down the sloping site and excavated a generous grotto. During the process, we realized we could remove the stone in blocks rather than in small fragments, the usual manner of excavation in Dade County.

Subsequent excavations eventually led to a deep pond, massive stone islands, and a thirteen-foot overhanging bluff sculpted out of bedrock. The pond is actually the water table; it fluctuates from season to season and tide to tide. Kingfishers, herons, and hawks stalk crustaceans and fish, while flocks of migratory fowl linger in the trees and open spaces. Pleasant water sounds offer surprises from unexpected places. A wispy twenty-foot cascade tumbles down a verdant cliff into a man-made sinkhole.

The bottom of the property once bordered wetlands and red mangrove forests. Fill and monoliths from the pond dig were used in landforms throughout the garden, creating privacy and providing drama. The plantings are mostly indigenous with cypress, pond apples, and red mangrove in the main pond as well as in the pond basin four feet above.

Accent plants including the sculptural kapok, South American oil palm, talipot, and Bailey palm from Cuba, to name a few, are distributed among the thick indigenous species. Clearings accentuate the sky and allow light penetration. From a rooftop tower at the crest of the hill are visible glimpses of the distant bay. The evening flights of Everglades birds heading for their nightly mangrove roosts animate the expansive window to the sky, and there is no better place from which to watch a lunar eclipse on a frigid Florida winter night.

The entry to the garden is sited between sculptural live oak trees; Florida wildflowers and silver saw palmettos grow beneath a towering American oil palm; an oolite limestone bluff and pond were once concealed by a gently sloping lawn.

PREVIOUS PAGE A springlike cascade tumbles into the main pond.

Cascades, streams, and basins are fed by a two-horsepower pump; the upper pond basin was detailed to create a primitive, agrarian feeling; massive boulders sculpted from oolitic limestone bedrock were influenced by formations in Roberto Burle Marx's gardens.

Carved stone monoliths are placed among indigenous flowering shrubs and wildflowers; a retaining wall comprised of oolite boulder monoliths creates a livable perch at the site of the original excavation for the residence's construction.

We purchased this 12,000-square-foot property as an investment. Our renovation started with the house, an 800-square-foot 1940s bungalow. The design was intentionally minimal, because the residence would be demolished in future plans. We removed sections of wall and added two expanses of sliding glass doors to open the limited common living spaces to the garden. Then we installed privacy fences and indigenous buffer planting. The side-yard building setback is seven feet, which allowed us to construct a tall wall to screen the neighboring one-story residence.

When Debra and I separated, I settled here for two years. The living/work space opened to a large wooden deck shaded by a reed mat suspended from cables. I lived an indoor/outdoor existence, and the softness of the garden provided a much-needed sanctuary. My philosophy for creating gardens had evolved after designing the Ward garden, where I placed almost all the emphasis on creating habitat using indigenous plants. I had no desire to mow lawns or hear blowers; I wanted to see birds and animals.

I had fun with the pool, focusing on the sculptural possibilities of combining the pool and screening wall. Although exaggerated in scale, the modulated massing of the floating wall sections is proportional to the garden and the anticipated new residence I had designed. Broken into three distinct volumes, the zigzag geometry contrasts with the sinuous shape of the pool coping opposite.

Light and soft sounds emanate from the vertical slot fountain elements in each wall section. A simple single-horsepower pump feeds the three elevated weirs; the pull of gravity does the rest. The sloping face of each chute's surface was hand-chiseled to encourage the passing water to leap and dance.

The wildness of the garden is a perfect counterpoint to the visual strength of the pool/fountain wall. Luis Barragán's influence is evident, as is Burle Marx's. Returning home one day I was greeted by a hawk perched overhead in a gumbo limbo tree. Due to the rural character of the property, the local children called it the Cuban Farm.

Florida Keys plants interlock to create a soft texture; water tumbles from one of the three slot fountains in the sculptural wall; the tripartite wall conceals an adjacent residence.

PREVIOUS PAGE The colored wall floats above the waterline and a continuous coping that provides a safe hand grip and visually lightens the wall's mass.

Plantings outside the privacy fence, like all species in this garden, are indigenous and chosen for their textures and hues; the intense green of Christmas berry complements the tones of the sculptural screening wall.

# JOHN EVANS AND GUY ROSS GARDEN

Key West, Florida | 2001–2002

John Evans and Guy Ross commissioned us to design a recently purchased plot of land north of their pool garden and residence, designed by architect Tom Pope. They asked us to procure twelve matching Florida royal palms to extend an allée from two existing trees. This allée would terminate at an intimately scaled fountain.

They were also interested in developing a flexible space able to accommodate large gatherings for fund-raising events. We suggested a water wall and a spatial rather than an axial organization. This concept honored and abstracted the Zen detailing of a Japanese waterfall and stream they had a liking for. Large boulders anchor the ten-by-thirty-foot water wall structure, and the randomly stepped cascades and planters are veneered with hand-chiseled stone rescued from the flooding of the Yangtze River Valley in China.

Although minimal and contemporary, the garden has a formality and symmetry that acts as a counterpoint to the residence, a Key West Victorian. The expansive central lawn is flanked by two other spaces of generous scale. The size of the royal palms is mediated by the introduction of rows of Cuban sabal palms. We tucked intimate spaces for food preparation and bar setups in secondary garden spaces at the periphery. The turf surface can be covered by plywood and tents for special occasions and charity events. A bamboo thicket behind the water wall blocks views of a thirty-foot-tall house across the street, and dense plantings of indigenous trees and understory shrubs screen the numerous adjacent residences that would otherwise loom over the space.

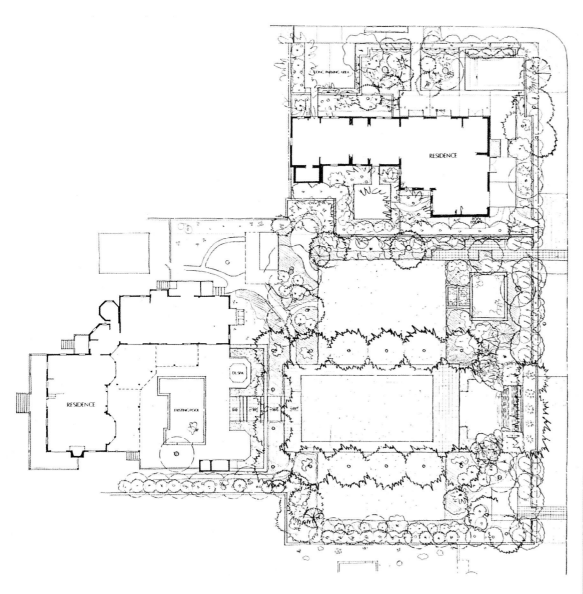

The site plan shows the residence and the guest house; the water wall contains the equipment vault and supports planters.

PREVIOUS PAGE The stepped weirs refer to a waterfall in Kyoto.

The view from the pool terrace takes in the garden
room and a distant elevated patio; bamboo
behind the water wall hides a two-story residence.

# ANAGRETHEL AND SAMUEL LEWIS GARDEN

Panama City, Panama | 2002–2005

When we first became involved with this project, the property was little more than a vast muddy set of slopes. Convenient to yet removed from the frenetic energy of Panama City, the dramatic piece of land had never been seriously considered for development. Our clients saw an opportunity to re-create in large scale the ambience of their weekend retreat on Isla Contadora, located in the Pearl Islands off the coast. The building site posed considerable challenges not only because of the topography but also due to the configuration of the lot.

The building plans, by architect Alvaro Gonzalez, Anagrethel's father, were finalized before the site plan was fully developed, so we proposed certain revisions to work with the landscape features of the site. We redirected the climbing entrance drive, bending it around an existing elephant's ear tree. We also suggested a small-scale pavilion pulled away from the body of the building in lieu of the grand porte-cochere in Gonzalez's scheme. Our intention was to float the pavilion in a lush tropical garden, creating planting areas to visually diminish the scale of the structure. The pavement beneath the pavilion roof is articulated with local stone in an axial pattern that draws the eye toward a multilevel reflection pond and a quiet waterfall enveloped in ferns.

Boulders strewn over the site lend credence to the organically shaped water elements and provide a visual foil to the scale of the architecture. The residence is three stories on the approach side, but four stories on the pool side, and the guest suite on the lowest level required a retaining wall to accommodate the grade change. We expanded the garden area by the guest quarters, adding a generous fish/turtle pond and water bowl cascade. The wall and eight-foot-diameter bowl are veneered with porous pebbles, which are ideal for supporting vegetation.

A proposed entertainment pavilion/gym occupied our preferred site for the main swimming pool, so we suggested pushing that building, which we ultimately designed, to the periphery of the property, behind a huge mango tree. The bathroom, gym, and spa share a generous covered terrace, and the roof is detailed as a planter to help the building blend into its surroundings. The vista from the gym takes in a long, shallow lounge pool accessible from the covered terrace, which provides a path to the spa and main pool beyond.

Nurseries of the kind common in the United States do not exist in Panama, so Anagrethel and I selected the plants from roadside family concessions. These were augmented by palms harvested from the family's other properties and a nursery that specializes in palms. The intentionally nonformal geometry of the garden is the perfect complement to the residence. It is a garden designed for a difficult site that offers comfort, diversity, and discovery.

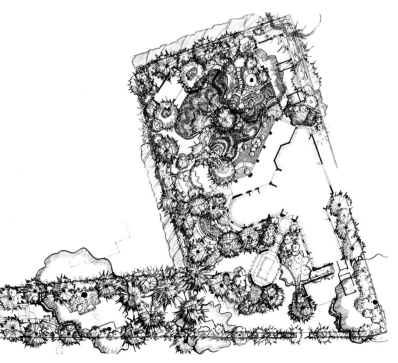

The plan for the three-quarter-acre site shows the residence and the drop-off pavilion; leading up to the gatehouse are panels of local stone articulated at a domestic scale; the pavilion is surrounded by a luxuriant garden; the axial view from the front door terminates in a shallow, heavily planted reflection pond.

PREVIOUS PAGE The minimal driveway paving, like other elements in the garden, is composed of local stone.

OVERLEAF The rainfall and rich soil of Panama foster rapid growth; Cryptanthus curls around a stone at the base of the water bowl; a Fiji Island palm emerges from the garden next to the entry drive; a path leads to the pool garden; an indigenous Kapok tree replaced an elephant's ear tree that did not survive the construction process.

The view from the great room of the main living level centers on the eight-foot-diameter water bowl and its twelve-foot cascade to the pond below; a shallow pool is one of the many water features in the garden; the guest suite has a view of the fish/turtle pond below the water bowl.

We designed the entertainment pavilion to meld into the landscape; the route from the covered terrace on the main floor to the pool level travels through a garden overlook, which houses pool and fountain equipment; the boulders and stone finish of the pool and deck create a sense of permanence.

# CASA MORADA

The challenge of Casa Morada was creating a relaxing, tropical resort–like atmosphere on a limited budget. Hotshot New York hoteliers were seeking to turn a partially renovated 1950s-era resort on Florida Bay into a cutting-edge, memorable experience in the Florida Keys. The two existing hotel buildings, essentially an old motor lodge, had no curb appeal, an excess of asphalt, poor circulation, and not a hint of inspiration.

The first step in transforming this sixteen-room hotel into a striking and unforgettable hideaway was reorganizing vehicular and pedestrian circulation. We reduced the impact of automobiles on the property by half by placing parking in convenient yet unobtrusive areas of the 1.7-acre site. The appearance of these areas is softened by removing the pavement or covering it with sand. The center of what used to be a vast asphalt parking lot is now an intimate garden space defined by three cast-in-place painted-concrete monoliths. Their dramatic architectural presence has become the hotel's visual signature. The lobby, which was moved to the back of the building, provides a view across the garden to Florida Bay. A trellis over a boardwalk along the north side of the building establishes a logical path that guides guests from the parking areas along a sandy lane.

For the most part, we used plants indigenous to the Florida Keys, which creates a veritable wildlife refuge. Once these were established, we removed a temporary low-emitting irrigation system. A rigid grid of Washingtonia palms defined the original waterside garden. We relocated these and other trees to generate maximum effect. In place of the palm grid, a limestone grotto imparts an intimate scale. A new garden thrives in the microclimate created by the grotto—this area is now the coolest part of the site—and benefits from the directed water drainage. Beyond the grotto, at the proposed location for a second pool, we built a grassy knoll that has become a popular spot for weddings. Fossilized keystone monoliths dug from the grotto define the space and offer a great place for viewing the sunset.

The existing pool, located on an island connected to the main property by a footbridge, was overdue for an update. Concrete, full of cracks and irregularities, covered 95 percent of the island. We demolished the old concrete and covered the island with 220 cubic yards of sand, linking the island to the mainland gardens. An almost unnoticeable concrete curb around the island's perimeter contains the new sand ground plane. An absolute minimum of new concrete decking around the pool and a matching coping produce a clean, bold look. Generous pool steps and waterline tile are simple and white, as is the pool's new coating. Beach-friendly plants grow in areas once covered by concrete.

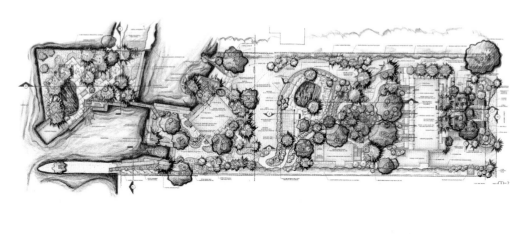

The pool island and the main property are presented in the plan; a monolith garden takes root on the site of a former parking lot; the main suite, over the lobby office, is called the Jungles Suite.

PREVIOUS PAGE Intense color links the monoliths, gumbo limbo trees, and *Aechmea* 'Dean' bromeliads.

Cuban petticoat palms emerge from indigenous
blanket flower; a trellis designed by Robert Werthamer
leads from the parking area to the office.

The keystone monoliths by the elevated knoll were excavated during the creation of the grotto; we removed or covered almost all of the concrete on the pool island; the view from the office takes in one of the many sandy paths in the garden.

Repeat clients remind us that our past designs are both meaningful and successful. In this case, our clients needed more space for themselves and their four young children. They wanted something on the scale of a botanical garden, with lots of color and a very tropical ambience.

The new house was set deep into the five-acre corner site, allowing us to establish an entrance that would provide privacy and security. The drive first crests a hill, giving an overview of the grounds, then meanders through the property. We designed numerous theatrical moments where the drive might narrow to pathlike dimensions, bringing the foliage close enough to touch, or broaden, to accommodate passing cars and emphasize the expansive garden space. (I learned this trick from Roberto Burle Marx, who always wondered at Americans and their uniform driveways.)

One of our biggest challenges was to eliminate the suburban feeling that typically results on a vast yet urban site. Our master plan calls for replacing an asphalt driveway with an elevated pedestrian plaza adjacent to the front door. Across the drive, under the shade of a mature live oak tree, the parents can relax while their children frolic on the great lawn. A fountain in a nearby pond sends up a single vertical stream, then splashes against a floating oolite limestone monolith covered with moss and ferns, providing spatial animation. In another area, an abstract bubbling spring rises from a stone shelf, appears to flow between floating monoliths, then spills into the pond below. Daily fish feedings are conducted from an oolite limestone bridge that spans the pond at its narrowest point.

The existing pool felt like a gigantic rock pile. We softened the stone by adding numerous plants that thrive in a minimal soil environment. Hurricanes had convinced the owners to eliminate the ubiquitous Florida screen enclosure around the pool, opening it up to the surrounding land-scape. We created space under the mature native trees and introduced an over-scaled Seminole chickee. This traditional Native American thatch pavilion, forty by twenty feet, was installed by local Miccosukee tribe members and is used for casual living.

The chickee also functions as the gateway to the property. A flagstone path links the various garden rooms, winding through numerous new planting beds and rising to become an elevated plaza adjoining the tennis court. The plaza/path, like the tennis court, may be transformed into a large dining patio. Then the path rises to the highest point of the site, a hill we created with fill from the lake's excavation. The view from this elevated position encompasses the great lawn and the pond beyond.

A mature live oak shades the adult lounge area adjacent to the children's play lawn; the single-jet fountain was inspired by one in Roberto Burle Marx's Camargo garden.

PREVIOUS PAGE Part of a trail that circumnavigates the entire site, a path leads from the guest parking area past a relocated wild tamarind and to the residence.

OVERLEAF Spineless agave and imperial bromeliads have a similar texture and scale; Hawaiian torch bougainvillea is planted at the side of the pond; an oolite bridge across the pond is the site for ceremonial fish feedings; water serves as the "mortar" for oolite stepping pads; pondside species were chosen for suitability in moist soils.

The existing pool was refinished to better suit the new garden; the Seminole chickee is an outdoor living room complete with bar and flatscreen television; our clients use the boat to maintain the water plants.

Designing and building gardens in the Florida Keys is always challenging and inspiring. Truly subtropical, the climate is defined by six months of little or no precipitation alternating with six months of rain, or hurricane season. Water for irrigation is expensive, coming by pipeline from Miami. Pre-pipeline inhabitants relied on cisterns or wells, but most of these wells have been infiltrated by salt water, rendering them useless.

We were brought into this project early on to advise our clients on the purchase of a site on Shark Key, ten miles east of Key West. The site we suggested on the otherwise barren, landfilled island is next to an earlier garden of ours. The dense natural plantings would provide a context to play off of and a habitat for local fauna. The property is divided into two separate flood zones, one allowing additional fill, the other prohibiting it. We suggested building the house over the portion of the lot where no fill was allowed, preserving the balance of the site for elevated gardens on a manipulated ground plane.

A gradual rise begins at an elevated parking court and climbs to the finish floor elevation eleven feet above. The ground plane beneath the residence is utilized for storage and shaded entertainment. From the street-side garden, views are into and through a lushly planted area to the bay beyond; the street is concealed by plantings and landforms. Guests pass through a bougainvillea-covered portal, traverse several garden levels, and finally reach the generous, continuous veranda of the residence. The axial organization of the entry walk relates to the symmetry of the architecture yet appears organic and relaxed.

Boulders carved out of the local fossilized coral-reef limestone, or keystone, shore up the sometimes radical grade changes. Except for the concrete pavers in the parking court and driveway, keystone in various forms is the hardscape material of choice throughout the garden.

The pool garden above the entry gardens is multileveled. The upper pool deck provides for a dramatic water view. Adjacent to the master bedroom wing is an elevated sculpture garden. Verandas flank both sides of the narrow, one-story, plantation-style residence, which from the water appears to be two stories high. From inside and from the veranda, the ground plain is invisible, the flats of Florida Bay stretch to the horizon, and the feeling is that of being on a boat.

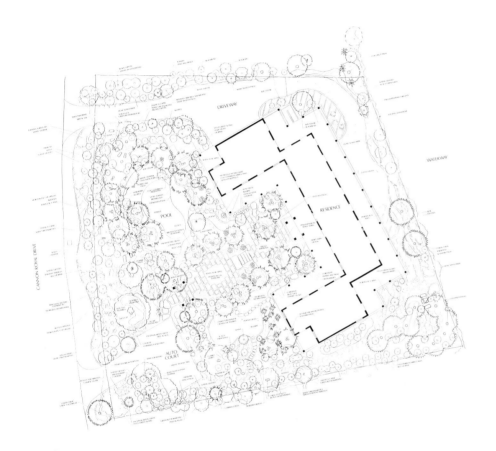

Most of the garden, as delineated in the plan, is on the landward, leeward side of the residence; a rare white silk floss tree from Brazil and a bull thatch palm from Cuba frame the path to the pool area; the detail of the garden portal mimics that of the multilevel residence designed by Tom Pope.

PREVIOUS PAGE Zoysia grass and keystone slabs define the open space before the portal.

The garden portal is entwined with bougainvillea;
the lower terrace is poised between the pool
garden and the master bedroom sculpture garden.

*Aechmea blanchetiana* 'Orange Form' from Brazil grows near the master bedroom wing; the view from the master bedroom takes in the entry garden and the pool garden; keystone is used in many areas of the garden, including the steps to the master bedroom garden.

Drought-tolerant bromeliads provide color and texture; the
sculpture garden outside the master bedroom looks toward the
pool garden; keystone flagstone borders the dark gray pool.

# STONE REEF HOUSE GARDEN

Key Largo, Florida | 2002–2004

Most buildings in coastal Florida are required to be elevated to a certain height above sea level. Creating gardens for elevated buildings calls for a proficiency uncommon in other parts of the country. For this winter residence at the Ocean Reef Club, the house had to be raised ten feet above the existing grade. Planting restrictions in the eighteen-foot side yards, established to preserve neighboring houses' water views, created another set of obstacles.

The client, a nature enthusiast, had grown up in nearby Coconut Grove and wanted his garden to blend the Everglades and the coast while providing for his two favorite hobbies: bird-watching and kayaking. Our objectives were to construct a natural habitat and wildlife refuge and to ensure the homeowner's privacy within the sterile, suburban neighborhood.

We first suggested adding a veneer of local oolite limestone to the exterior of the building to connect house and land. In lieu of the ubiquitous circular driveway, an entrance path weaves from the street through dense indigenous vegetation over Florida keystone slabs. A vine-covered wooden trellis atop outsized stone columns extends from the front door to the landing at the base of the entry steps, softening the building's mass.

On the water side, the elevated pool area is integrated with the garden to unify building and land. Mature palm trees in recessed planters set flush with the deck add to the illusion that the house is grounded; the boundary between the pool and the Atlantic is blurred with an infinity edge. An immense fire bowl seems to float in the pool and adds drama to the black void of the nighttime view.

The bold columns and vine pergola of the entry are repeated on the ocean side. Keystone slabs, which appear to float in a water garden, connect the guest room to the pergola. Outside the kitchen, a cozy covered pavilion overlooks the pool and the ocean beyond; it is the perfect place to watch the sunrise with coffee in hand. Wooden stairs, articulated with a lounge and view platform midway, extend to the garden below. Oolite monoliths, some carved into planters, terrace down the back of the pool deck for a gradual passage to the garden path and the kayak launch site. Enveloped in mature trees, indigenous plants, and local stone, the house peeks out from what seems to be natural woodland and provides a sanctuary from which the family can enjoy both nature and the sea.

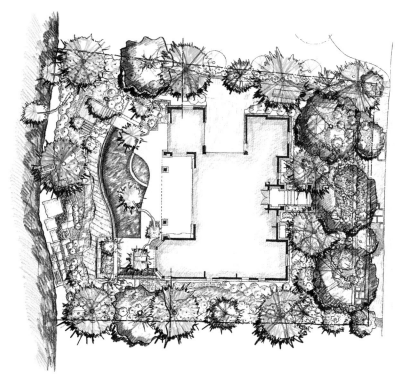

Required setbacks from the water's edge determined the shape of the pool, and required view corridors for the neighbors determined the side-yard plantings; a path of keystone slabs winds toward the front door; we designed the oolite lime-stone veneer for the residence as well as the matching trellis.

PREVIOUS PAGE A hammock of mostly Florida Keys native plants envelops the house, designed by architect Robert Wade.

The garden steps up from a zoysia terrace perfect for launching kayaks to a pool deck fifteen feet above sea level; the oolite boulders of the retaining wall were cut from the limestone bedrock of Dade County.

The water in the pool and the water in the ocean fuse to link garden and horizon; the pool pavilion extends the character of the architecture into the garden; the elevated pavilion provides a comfortable vantage point to enjoy a dramatic view.

# EL PALMAR

Our clients decided early on that they wanted their new house and garden to reflect the haciendas of their Cuban homeland, complete with royal palms, a generous lawn, and tropical textures. Designed by Cesar Molina, formerly of Molina & Narcisse, the tropical colonial–style architecture, with its covered verandas and buildings arranged to create integral garden spaces, is well suited to the subtropical climate.

Our first big gesture was to install a pedestrian-scale plaza outside the perimeter fence of the house proper. A sizeable trellis, set back fifty feet from the property line, runs perpendicular to the street and is covered with flowering vines that veil views of the house. Once inside the auto gate, cars are directed along a long natural drive that imparts the feeling of the approach to a rural estate. Since there was no budget for pavement, we excavated slightly to expose the oolite limestone bedrock, grinding it for a more even surface.

The two-and-a-half-acre corner lot offered numerous topographic challenges. Situated on the highest ridge in South Florida (in fact, just a short distance from the Ward garden), the property slopes gently from almost twenty feet to only four feet above sea level. The excavation for the foundation of the guesthouse, across the auto court from the main house, created a four-foot bluff, making the house appear awkwardly sited. To compensate, we reversed the slope of the hill away from the guesthouse, constructing an oolite limestone formation. We built a stream to cascade down the slope and over the top of the formation as a seemingly natural waterfall. Fill from the immense excavation contours the site, creating undulations that appear natural and setting up a wide variety of garden experiences. Fruit trees and indigenous plants along the periphery define a window to the sky and create habitat and privacy.

The random concrete panels from the entry plaza are repeated in the auto court. Offset with zoysia grass, they allow for the percolation of rainwater. In the center of the generous courtyard, a large rectangular oolite monolith carved on site to function as a bubbling water basin is flanked by red feather palms with vanda orchids attached to their trunks.

On the waterway side of the house, the pool, developed by Molina, is an extension of the architecture. The pool and garden patio are at the level of the house. Inside the pool, we added seat ledges, steps, and finishing that mimic the residence. Palms shade the pool and patios; pavement is minimized. Views across the pool area and down the long wide waterway influenced the placement of the widest portions of the pool deck. Between the pool pavilion and pool is a rectangular water garden with fish. The terraced lawn beyond the pool is sized to accommodate a tent for large parties. Past this, steps down to the boathouse and its parking court pass through oolite retention walls that convey the feeling of a grotto.

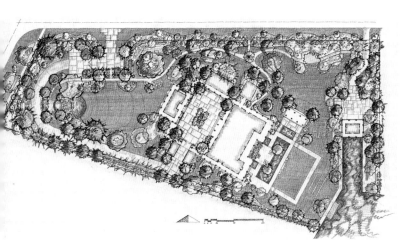

The distinct garden spaces shown in the plan were tailored to the demands of the newly created topography; the guest house is visible across the water garden/grotto; we planted agaves to add drama to an existing multi-trunked baobab.

PREVIOUS PAGE Cliff date palms, collected on-site, are grouped atop the newly built oolite bluff.

OVERLEAF All species, except the baobab, were planted once the contours of the site were established.

The steps leading from a garden overlook were cut from bedrock; the courtyard fountain is a thirteen-foot-long oolite monolith; Bismarck palms sprout from the elevated pool deck; stepping pads and pool-deck veneer are both made of limestone.

# ALICIA ZIEGERT D'AGOSTINO AND FRANCO D'AGOSTINO GARDEN

Indian Creek Village, Florida | 2001–2004

Alicia Ziegert, a repeat client and knowledgeable plantswoman, called us in for the landscape of a residence she was renovating in Indian Creek Village. Rather than attempting to create an architectural presence where none existed, she proposed an extremely diverse botanical garden that would envelop the building.

Across the street was a golf course, and we decided to "borrow" the parklike setting for the new front garden. We established an axial view between the entry veranda and the golf course; the balance of the area is lushly planted with some of the many species requested by Alicia. The cobblestone driveway and parking court are generous but subtle.

In back, the residences across the narrow waterway are screened by a beach structure and a grove of palms. We added seat ledges, generous steps, tile, and fiber-optic lighting to the existing swimming pool. The geometry of the pool extends beyond an enlarged bridgelike deck to terminate at a water wall and fountain basin. A wide, stepped chute dematerializes the low wall, encouraging views into the garden beyond. Minimally detailed sitting-height planters, veneered with stone from the Florida Keys, contain palms and vines that mask the walls of the house.

Water also plays a role in the interior spaces. A grotto-like fountain and pond is visible from the glass hallway between the covered terrace at poolside and the master bedroom suite. Each adjacent room is oriented to a distinct fountain element, all sculpted from the same oolite limestone of the beach pavilion and Alicia's address plaque.

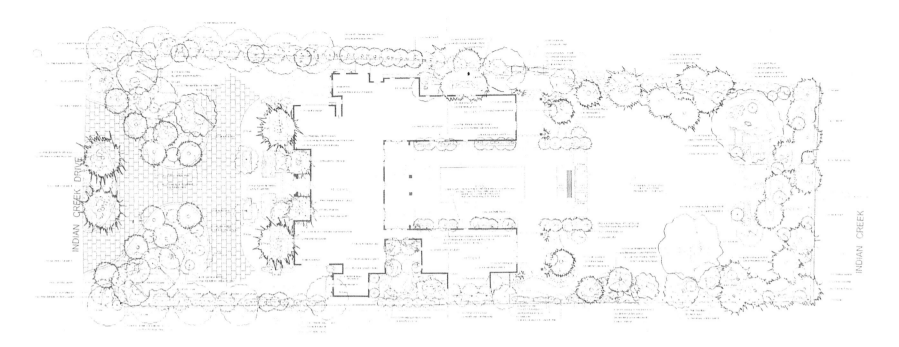

The plan consists of three distinct garden rooms: front garden with cobblestone drive, pool area, and back garden along Indian Creek; the oolite plaque bears the name of the garden, and of Alicia's favorite palm, Palmyra; Palmyras and tropical blue bamboo frame the entrance portal.

PREVIOUS PAGE The fountain and the distant pavilion are new, while the pool was extensively renovated.

Keystone-veneered planters float above the pool deck;
the rustic beach pavilion shares a site by the waterway
with a boat dock and barbecue grill.

The pavilion can accommodate up to twenty people; the poolside loggia overlooks a fishpond/fountain; the view from the library includes a wall fountain and sculpture ledge.

Gentle sound emanates from the stepped fountain, which directs a wide chute toward the pool and a narrow cascade to the back garden; the palm grove along Indian Creek conceals residences but permits glimpses of the water.

# JULIE AND JACK MILLER GARDEN

Stuart, Florida | 2003–2005

Many of the plants I use are grown by my friend Jack Miller, one of the owners of Botanics Wholesale Nursery in Homestead, Florida. When Jack and his wife, Julie, built a new residence on the Indian River, a wide section of the Intercoastal Waterway, they asked me to help with the garden design. It was important to screen the similarly sited adjacent residences and to showcase Jack's extensive plant inventory.

The lot is long and narrow, 100 by 800 feet, with the Florida vernacular–style house sited at the waterfront building setback line to maximize river views. The sandy beach was fortified with a caprock bulkhead, and the pool shell and front property line wall had already been established. Few trees existed on-site, but a grove of mature Enterolobium, a deciduous sculptural tree from Central America, graced the property to the south.

We first removed a portion of the front property line wall to allow a serpentine rather than an axial approach to the residence. The drive winds through a grove of sabal palms, Florida's state tree, and around a slightly elevated water garden, straightening to emphasize a long vista through the Enterolobium grove. The drive then circles a deep grotto and finally arrives at the auto court, paved in the stained concrete of the pool deck. Repetition and simplification are guiding principles in our designs.

Composed primarily of sustainable indigenous plants, the garden is rich in botanical diversity. Paths invite exploration and facilitate maintenance. The pool garden is animated by a higher than usual bench from which water cascades. The deck provides poolside lounging while delivering views to the river beyond.

The Miller property exemplifies my philosophy of regionalism in gardening. A garden in Florida should not look like a garden in Hawaii, or in Bali or Fiji. Florida plants and materials should dominate, while non-invasive ornamental species from other tropical and subtropical areas may play a secondary role.

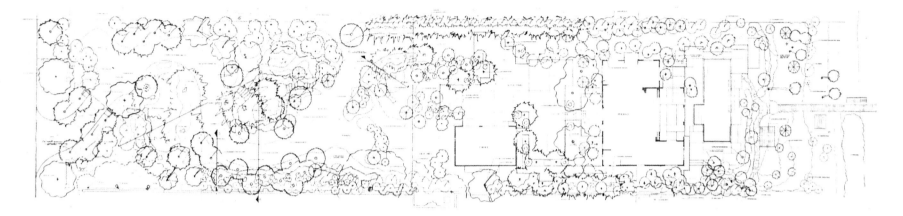

The winding driveway is an important feature of the plan; the crushed shell of the drive terminates in a stained concrete plaza between house and garage; our typical step sequence—two steps followed by a landing—was inspired by Luis Barragán.

PREVIOUS PAGE The driveway winds through and around various garden spaces.

Sabal palms, which must be supported during
the first hurricane season after planting, lean over
the grotto; old man palms from Cuba, agaves,
and bromeliads are placed to emphasize the rare
species grown and sold by our clients; the site
of the water garden was once barren sand.

We designed the bench fountain with its subtle cascade; plantings screen neighboring houses and docks, but not the Indian River.

# SUSAN HENSHAW JONES AND RICHARD EATON GARDEN

Key West, Florida | 2003–2005

Susan Henshaw Jones and Richard Eaton purchased this Key West property as a warm-weather family getaway. The couple wanted to integrate the garden and the interior of the suburban, 1940s one-story residence, a tactic they had noted in other projects of ours.

We did studies to develop an ideal floor plan, taking into account site limitations and zoning regulations. Along with architect Rob DeLaune, we developed a central living space that spans from property line to property line. Fountains animate both sides of the living space. Wide expanses of pocket doors, normally kept open, erase the separation between indoors and out. We recommended building a swimming pool in place of the asphalt circular driveway, converting the garage into a master bedroom suite, and integrating garden atriums into the plan.

Garden architecture enriches the entrance sequence and provides a strong presence to contrast with the lush, mostly indigenous plantings. The carport defines the point of entry. An aluminum trellis suspended between the carport and the residence shelters the entry walk. Its pivoting gate allows views into the garden. The walk is transformed into a series of slabs that float above a small water garden. A fountain fed by a one-half-horsepower pump tumbles into the water garden.

The plain side elevation of the building is tucked behind a large garden wall. Perforations of various sizes in the wall frame garden views from the children's bedrooms and either restrict or enable movement. By the pool, the wall turns to become an outdoor shower.

The reflective surface of the swimming pool is a window to the sky. Privacy from the two-story residences across the street is provided by various layers of indigenous trees; these were selected to reach a dense, mature height of twenty feet and to provide habitat for local birds and butterflies. The master bedroom suite has multiple garden views and an open feeling throughout. A private atrium adjacent to the master bathroom and shower allows for light and garden views to penetrate the core of the rooms, creating a seamless connection between indoor and outdoor spaces.

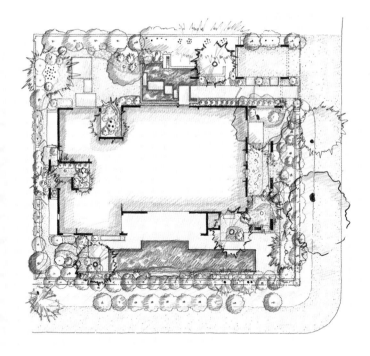

Indicated in the plan are two bodies of water, including the front pool, which replaced a circular driveway; the entry sequence consists of carport, trellis, and gate; the rear wall of the house was extended to become a supporting wall of the trellis.

PREVIOUS PAGE The trellis and water wall are characteristic of the garden architecture.

OVERLEAF The water garden and water wall are only ten feet from the rear property line.

Travertine panels float in the water garden, providing a refuge for fish; the trellis is enveloped in herald's trumpet and Jacquemontia vines; the master bedroom looks out to the swimming pool.

Water cascades down a bush-hammered concrete chute and into the pool; layers of trees mask the residences across the street; the decking for the fifty-foot pool is kept to a minimum.

Judy Blume, world-renowned writer, and her philanthropist husband were initially attracted to this Florida property because of the garden, which we had built for the previous owner, a close friend. They particularly wanted to expand the indoor/outdoor flow of the spaces to make the house more transparent yet still very private.

The design team—Judy, architect Tom Pope, designers Roman & Williams, and us—decided to relocate the equipment/electrical room at the core of the living space to the roof and to create a new master bathroom with a private secure garden and outdoor shower. The garden would double the living space of both the bedroom and the bathroom. Elements such as the carport, walls, murals, and covered porches were retained, but the eclectic tastes of the new owners—dark wood and interesting sculptural accents—are evident throughout.

We removed a play lawn and replaced it with more plantings. Dark gravel on the ground absorbs glare and needs no watering; a temporary floor can be installed for parties and games. Quiet views for contemplation abound. We softened the colors, adding grays and greens to the stone platform of the covered terrace and masonry walls. Hardscape and softscape were selected with durability in mind: numerous recent hurricanes had emphasized that indigenous and salt-tolerant plants survived better than exotics.

Our favorite contribution, however, was in positioning the master bathroom mirrors to reflect the garden. Nature permeates the interior. The dark, stacked-stone shower wall imparts intimacy. The bananas embrace, while the thorny wall-top planters sustain privacy. The garden now has a completely different spirit, one that corresponds to the personalities of Judy and her husband.

The garden, originally designed for Steve and Dale Dunn, was renovated with an eye toward minimal maintenance; the gravel surface by the loggia can be covered with plywood flooring to accommodate dancing or ping-pong.

PREVIOUS PAGE The stainless-steel chute, used daily for showering al fresco, provides a dramatic cascade for special occasions.

The soft colors of the covered loggia and other elements in the garden are tailored to Judy Blume's preferences; the entry shelter is supported by three posts and has a skylight; outside the master bathroom is a protected garden.

OVERLEAF The poolside planter/fountain wall, which screens a neighboring house, is the backdrop for a ceramic mural by Debra Yates.

The pool steps are a pleasant place to lounge; the ledge at the base of the mural, shaded by a native silver saw palmetto, is a favored resting spot; the guest house and writing studio are beyond the mass of palms at the end of the pool.

Shimmering sand beaches stretch for miles along the Atlantic Ocean in South Florida. In this winter playground of hotels and condominiums, private beachfront residences are rare. Yet here one homeowner found his personal slice of paradise in a nondescript house overlooking the sea in Golden Beach.

The long narrow lot, 60 by 270 feet, did not have much room for landscaping, although it was desperately needed. Along the south face of the building, we eliminated parking and a proposed covered walkway. Instead, we redirected circulation from the auto court to the front door through a linear garden. A gently ramped travertine path, enveloped in lush plantings, gradually reveals the Atlantic Ocean, a stunning surprise. The door is flanked by salt-tolerant Maling bamboo. A large window next to the entry brings this garden indoors, as gentle shadows of the bamboo dance across the room.

Parallel to the path, a sleek cascading stream flows from the entrance to the auto court. The two-tiered water feature masks the sounds of the busy street and comes alive at night with thousands of tiny fiber-optic lights. Along the house, plantings are layered in various volumes and feature a variety of native and exotic species. On the other side of the path, in a restrictive three-foot-wide planting space at the southernmost edge of the property, we installed a dense buffer of mostly salt-tolerant Florida natives including sabal palms, pigeon plums, silver buttonwoods, and Jamaican caper. Their staggered heights screen the neighboring house, which is less than ten feet away. Bromeliads and orchids grow on tree trunks, adding color to the predominantly green palette.

Beyond the entry, the path descends to the beach, pausing at the travertine pool deck. The generously scaled infinity-edge pool underscores the horizon. Nighttime fiber-optic lighting produces a peaceful glow, out of view of the nesting sea turtles on the beach. We added coconut and bottle palms seaside and planted the dune with native species including agaves, yuccas, sea oats, and dune sunflower.

Light streams into the north side of the house through floor-to-ceiling windows, which balance the proportions of the room and incorporate the ten-foot-wide side yard into the interior space. In this narrow area we designed a bilevel travertine shelf to display pottery, sculpture, and plants. Behind the shelves are thin, multi-trunked Everglades palms.

Often our best solutions result from working under very tight constraints. On this limited site we juxtaposed elements of water, sound, light, and color while keeping hardscape materials bold and minimal. We endeavored to strike a balance of scale to link the natural and man-made environments.

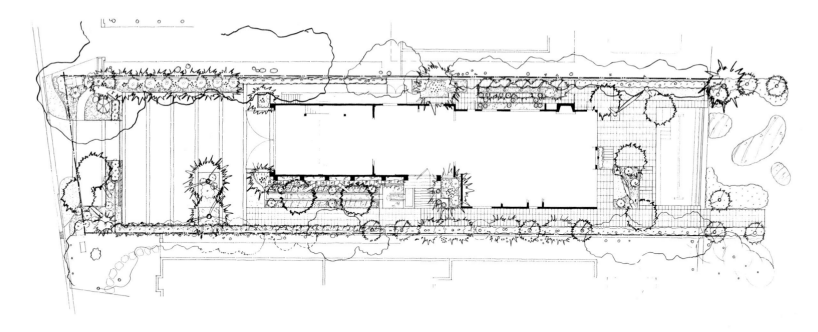

The narrow site accommodates a generous auto court, slim entrance garden, slimmer north garden, and pool/beach area; the elevated deck sets the stage for an infinity-edge pool and keeps sand on the beach; carefully placed trees shield almost all of the house from the busy highway.

PREVIOUS PAGE Coconut, Everglades, and Bismarck palms provide scale to the entry path.

The view along the travertine path links the Atlantic Ocean to the entry sequence; the garage and vine trellis repeat the organic pattern of the stainless-steel auto and pedestrian gates; the stainless-steel trellis accommodates a newly planted palm.

The window and exterior display shelf blur the boundaries between inside and outside; plants and objects on the shelf may be changed for variety; fiber-optic lights enliven the stream at night.

The pool interior is patterned with tiles that gradually change from light to dark, emulating the Atlantic's transition from shallow to deep; the view from the lower level of the house shows the platform steps and infinity-edge pool.

# LYNNE AND CHIP SHOTWELL GARDEN

Naples, Florida | 2004–2007

Lynne and Chip Shotwell are fellow admirers of my late mentor and friend, Roberto Burle Marx. The couple had built a modern house in the unlikely locale of Naples, Florida, which is teeming with Mediterranean-inspired design, and they wanted a garden to match. The Shotwells, avid fishermen and garden enthusiasts, also requested botanical diversity and convenient access to the water for their Florida "fish camp."

The owners specifically chose the long, low, 60,000-square-foot lot for the protected waters that could accommodate their 74-foot sport-fishing boat. It was vital to plan the garden with adequate turning radii for boat trailers and drivable paths to supply the boat and boathouse for deep-sea excursions. We used natural stone—green Brazilian quartzite in the front garden and driveway and limestone in the rear and side yards—for the hard surfaces to impart a pedestrian scale to the entire site.

A slight, newly created hill at the entrance immediately reveals a long vista to a waterway that leads to the Gulf of Mexico. A bulkhead of immense limestone caprock boulders enlarges the usable garden space. We screened unpleasant intrusions from view and contoured the land to introduce an abundance of garden experiences. Hills and ledges deflect rain to shallow basins and grottoes, storing and recycling the rainfall for the benefit of water-loving plants. Paths invite exploration, luring occupants and visitors to private patios and contemplative spaces while facilitating ease of maintenance. A pocket beach along the new bulkhead affords fishing or lounging.

We borrowed from Mark Leonardi's architecture in the design of a pergola between the parking court and the house, banishing the presence of automobiles from the entry garden sequence. A floating slab path of green Brazilian quartzite leads from the pergola to the entry court and front door. The limestone entry court crosses a bridge over a fishpond where a stone water wall and an upper reflection weir double the visual impact. Limestone-covered planters on the sides of the walkway support thatch palms, lignum vitae, and bromeliads, while juncus springs from the water basin.

Plants with permanent colorful foliage appeal to Lynne's love of color. Blooming tropical accents such as ground orchids and bromeliads, in combination with wildflowers and tuberous begonias, add generous floral masses. We relocated large trees to more advantageous positions and added others to create an overstory canopy beneath which a rich variety of shade-loving plants can thrive.

Natural stone, organic geometry, and minimalist details make garden and architecture seem as if they were drawn by the same hand. So while the placid Gulf waters entice the Shotwells out most days for some angling, their garden is their anchor onshore.

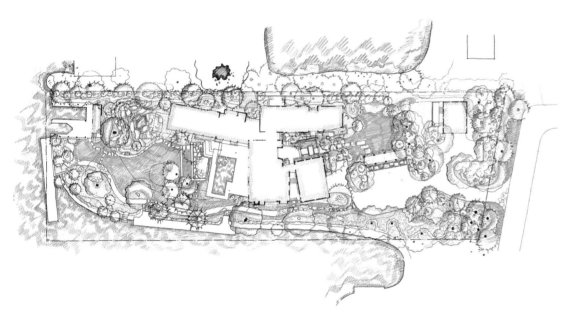

The garden was designed with access to the water in mind; Brazilian quartzite panels lead from the pergola to the residence; the grade beneath the master bedroom balcony was lowered to accentuate the cantilevered element.

PREVIOUS PAGE A crushed-shell path leads through black olive trees.

Brazilian quartzite reappears throughout the garden, notably in the fountain weir and water wall; the weir visually doubles the water garden; the path extends the primary circulation corridor of the residence into the garden.

A Brancusi-inspired fountain stands by the entry pergola; *Aechmea carioca* bromeliads and spineless agave bloom above a conch shell; portea bromeliads from Roberto Burle Marx's gardens were originally collected on an excursion into the wilds of Brazil; the caprock bulkhead allowed us to expand the garden.

# TERENCE RILEY AND JOHN BENNETT GARDEN

Roberto Burle Marx is the only landscape designer/artist to have had a solo exhibition at the Museum of Modern Art in New York. So Terence Riley, director of the Miami Art Museum and formerly chief curator in MoMA's Department of Architecture and Design, has a special appreciation for Burle Marx's work, as does his partner, architect John Bennett. They asked us to create the garden for their new Mies-inspired residence, which they designed with John Keenen of K/R. We were excited by the strong, clean architecture, minimal yet visually rich interiors, and fusion of interior and exterior spaces.

Although the available planting areas were small, they are integral to the overall ambiance. Street side, the entrance garden had been expanded by the elimination of a parking space. Here we added simple mass plantings of contrasting textures. Inside the high privacy wall, the plantings are more lush and tropical. For this garden, we hoisted Everglades palms over the wall and reassembled them as a mass, attaching orchids to their thin trunks. Natural light filters into the interiors through this grove.

For the bedroom wing, it was important to provide shade. Here, in the most tropical area of the garden, we used cabada palms, lady palms, and heliconias. Finally, we sheltered Riley and Bennett's central pool garden from a two-story residence less than thirty feet away with masses of bamboo and a couple of mature sabal palms.

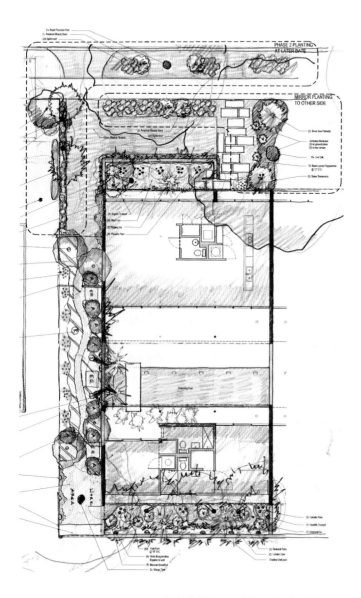

Each distinct area of the garden is defined by the architecture; a large live oak in the street-side garden shades the entrance to the house and that of its twin.

PREVIOUS PAGE Climbing fig on the privacy wall will come to resemble a clipped hedge.

Lady palms and cabada palms shade the bedrooms;
the interior spaces and the pool garden have views
to multiple landscaped areas; a wall of windows barely
separates a garden room from the living room.

The guest bedroom looks across the pool to the main
living space; the pool reflects the dense jungle
installed to screen the adjacent two-story residence.

# ELLA FONTANALS-CISNEROS ROOFTOP GARDEN

Coconut Grove, Florida | 2007–2008

Ella Fontanals-Cisneros, design advocate, art collector, philanthropist extraordinaire, persuaded us to take on her private residential garden. "The sky's the limit," she said. And she meant it. The site is thirty-four stories above Coconut Grove's main boulevard, across from Sailboat Bay.

The views from the 2,543-square-foot, L-shaped rooftop are spectacular (although on the scary side for some). We developed the program for the garden with Ella and her Spanish interior designer, Luis Bustamante: a cozy, secure space with human-scale proportions; plantings as lush as the high winds and glaring sun would allow; low-maintenance and drought-tolerant landscape materials; accommodation for intimate groups and for gatherings of fifty or more.

We lengthened the fifteen-foot-square pool, correcting its proportions, and added a wide lounging ledge. Stepped ipê platforms, which diminish the pool's obtrusive mass, provide water access. The dimensions of the pool are expressed in the adjacent stone water wall. Thousands of fiber optic filaments placed between the stacked stones twinkle at night, mimicking the city's lights. An infinity edge pulls the pool's surface taut. Water cascades over the edge, splashing down a vertical tiled surface into a basin four feet below. Two massive columns that are expressed on the bayfront facade of the building rise above roof level, and we sculpted them to allow for better circulation around the pool.

The ipê wood of the pool shell, elevated deck, and platform steps creates a datum line on the walls and wraps a new storage cabinet, which doubles as an elevated planter, as well as a private service kitchen with dumbwaiter near the dining area. Over the dining and kitchen area, we installed an aluminum trellis in the vocabulary of the building and a retractable awning.

At the elbow of the L-shaped garden is a snug sitting area. Benches and planters keep occupants a safe distance—actual and psychological—from the roof's edge. The pavement is articulated with patterns and textures seemingly connected with the earth's ground plane, and the aluminum finish of the custom planters matches the building's detailing. On the eighteen-foot wall adjacent to the main access to the rooftop is a stainless-steel cable grid that will support fragrant flowering vines. A panel of tillandsia, designed by Jennifer Davit, floats in its center.

Water cascades down the stone wall and into the pool—
but only when the wind is not too high; the trellis
shelters an outdoor kitchen and dining area; the ipê deck and
platforms unite the mass of the pool with the garden.

PREVIOUS PAGE The view toward downtown Miami is
one of the defining features of the roof garden.

OVERLEAF The new trellis imparts a domestic scale
to the dining and kitchen area; the kitchen walls
and storage cabinet are enfolded in ipê slats.

Jennifer Davit's tillandsia panel is the centerpiece of the wall at the garden entry; a low planter grounds the bench; pebbles around the concrete pavers recall the details of ground-level gardens; the pots at the door to the roof garden conceal lighting and speakers.

# ACKNOWLEDGMENTS

First and foremost, I would like to thank all of the clients who have graciously allowed me to share their private gardens on these pages. Without their support and the support of many others, I would be merely a dreamer.

I don't do these gardens alone; there are myriad people involved. I want to recognize my staff, both those who have assisted me in the past and those who make my life easier now. Special thanks to Stan Matthews, a dear friend and master garden builder. His company, Plant Creations, has implemented the bulk of the gardens shown in this book. Dave Schroeder, Stan's project foreman, is an invaluable asset. Don Trezona and his company, Gardenscapes, are also a joy to work with. Sean Jacobus, the legendary tree guru, supplied many of the specimen trees—some of them originally destined for Disney World—for my gardens.

My forte is designing, so it has been a challenge to produce the text for this book. I enlisted help from various individuals, including Anastasia Bowen, Eric Herman, Carol Pierce, Cynthia Shore, and my talented daughter, Amanda Jungles.

Finally, I am grateful to Gianfranco Monacelli, Andrea Monfried, Nicolas Rojas, Elizabeth White, and Stacee Lawrence of The Monacelli Press and John Clifford of Think Studio. Andrea polished my prose and offered timely, invaluable advice, and John understood my aesthetic sense intuitively and designed a beautiful, elegant volume.

Raymond Jungles is founder and proprietor of Raymond Jungles, Inc., established in 1983 and based in downtown Miami. Jungles graduated from the University of Florida in 1981.

   The work of Raymond Jungles, Inc., has appeared in numerous magazines and newspapers worldwide and in 1999 was the subject of the book *Ten Landscapes: Raymond Jungles*. Jungles, elected a fellow of the American Society of Landscape Architects in 2006, is a frequent lecturer and design jury member. He has won dozens of awards and has been named Landscape Architect of the Year by the Miami Chapter of the American Institute of Architects (2003) and distinguished alumnus by the University of Florida (2000). In 1991, he helped design and build the bromeliad sculpture in the Roberto Burle Marx exhibition at the Museum of Modern Art in New York, and he will design the 2009 Orchid Show for the New York Botanical Garden.

## RAYMOND JUNGLES, INC., 1981–2008

| | |
|---|---|
| Perla Aguayo | Jose Lopez |
| Zaida Alfaro | Maria Soledad Monsalve |
| Chris Alonso | Tyler Nielsen |
| Luis Aqui | David Odishoo |
| Andres Arcila | Bruce Ora |
| Luis Arencibia | Carol Pierce |
| Ted Baker | Erica Reid |
| Jared Beck | Craig Reynolds |
| Mauricio Del Valle | Alejandro Rodriguez |
| John Farrar | Cynthia Shore |
| Vincent Filigenzi | James "Jimmytico" Socash |
| Marcelo Garcia Ferrer | Carrie Steinbaum |
| Patrick Hodges | Jane Thurber |
| Justine Kwiatkowski | Cristina Urbina |

# PHOTOGRAPHY CREDITS

Unless credited below, all illustrations have been provided by Raymond Jungles, Inc. Numbers refer to page numbers. On pages 2, 3, 220, and 221, photo a is on the top left, photo b is on the top right, and so on.

JENNIFER ARCILA: 216, 217

BRENT BINGHAM: 132, 134 right, 135, 136, 137, 138, 139

STEVEN BROOKE: 2g

RICHARD FELBER: 2f, 2h, 3f, 3g, 18, 20 left, 21, 25, 76, 78, 81 right, 82, 96, 98 right, 99, 100 upper left, 100 upper right, 100 lower right, 101, 103 right, 104 right, 105, 106, 108 right, 109, 110, 111, 112 right, 113, 114, 116, 117, 118, 119, 120, 121, 125, 158, 160 lower, 161, 162, 163, 165, 176, 179, 180, 184, 185, 220c, 220f, 221b, 221c, 221f

HELEN FICKLING: 47, 69, 70, 73, 74 right, 75

ROGER FOLEY: 2b, 8–9, 34, 36 right, 37, 38, 39, 40, 41, 42, 46, 65, 80, 81 left, 83, 90, 93, 94, 95, 128, 129 right, 140, 142 right, 143, 144–45, 146, 147, 148, 150 lower, 152, 154, 155 left, 156, 157, 186, 188 lower, 189, 190, 191, 192, 193, 194, 195, 204, 208, 209, 210, 211, 212, 214, 218, 219, 220d

JERRY HARPUR: 44 right, 49, 58, 66–67, 130 left, 182–83

JACQUELINE M. KOCH: 63 left

HARUYOSHI ONO: 15

LANNY PROVO: 2a, 3a, 3b, 3c, 3d, 3h, 6–7, 22, 23, 24 left, 26, 28 right, 29, 30, 31, 32, 33, 44 left, 48, 52 lower, 53, 54, 55 upper left, 55 right, 56, 57, 60 right, 62, 74 left, 84, 166, 168 right, 170–71, 172, 174, 175, 220a, 220e, 220g, 220h, 221a, 221d, 221g, 221h

ANNIE SCHLECHTER: 207

CURTICE TAYLOR: 45, 50, 79, 122, 126, 127, 130 right, 131